DISCARDED

Feeling Happy

by Rosalyn Clark

BUMBA BOOKS™

LERNER PUBLICATIONS ◆ MINNEAPOLIS

Note to Educators:

Throughout this book, you'll find critical thinking questions. These can be used to engage young readers in thinking critically about the topic and in using the text and photos to do so.

Copyright © 2018 by Lerner Publishing Group, Inc.

All rights reserved. International copyright secured. No part of this book may be reproduced, stored in a retrieval system, or transmitted in any form or by any means—electronic, mechanical, photocopying, recording, or otherwise—without the prior written permission of Lerner Publishing Group, Inc., except for the inclusion of brief quotations in an acknowledged review.

Lerner Publications Company
A division of Lerner Publishing Group, Inc.
241 First Avenue North
Minneapolis, MN 55401 USA

For reading levels and more information, look up this title at www.lernerbooks.com.

Library of Congress Cataloging-in-Publication Data

Names: Clark, Rosalyn, 1990– author.
Title: Feeling happy / Rosalyn Clark.
Description: Minneapolis : Lerner Publications, [2017] | Series: Bumba books. Feelings matter | Audience: Ages 4–7. | Audience: K to grade 3. | Includes bibliographical references and index.
Identifiers: LCCN 2016059591 (print) | LCCN 2017012092 (ebook) | ISBN 9781512450255 (eb pdf) | ISBN 9781512433685 (lb : alk. paper) | ISBN 9781512455458 (pb : alk. paper)
Subjects: LCSH: Happiness in children—Juvenile literature. | Emotions—Juvenile literature.
Classification: LCC BF723.H37 (ebook) | LCC BF723.H37 C53 2017 (print) | DDC 152.4/2—dc23
LC record available at https://lccn.loc.gov/2016059591

Manufactured in the United States of America
1 – CG – 7/15/17

Expand learning beyond the printed book. Download free, complementary educational resources for this book from our website, www.lernerresource.com.

LERNER
SOURCE

Table of Contents

Feeling Happy

Happiness is a feeling.

What makes you happy?

Maybe you heard

a funny joke.

It made you smile

and laugh.

Laughing is a sign

you are happy.

Maybe there is a fun party.

You are happy to see your friends.

What else at a party could make you happy?

8

Maybe it is a sunny day.

You get to play at the park.

Maybe you are going on a field trip.

Field trips make learning fun.

Where might you go on a field trip?

Maybe you made a new friend.

Meeting people can be fun.

It makes you feel happy.

Doing something you enjoy

can make you happy.

Maybe you like to paint

or read.

You can help others feel happy.

You may see someone who is alone.

You can ask her to play with you.

Maybe you have a snack.

You can share it.

Sharing can make you

feel happy too.

What other things could you share with a friend?

Picture Quiz

Which child is happy? Point to that picture.

Picture Glossary

feeling

an emotion
or thought

field trip

when a group goes
to a place to see
things and learn

share

to divide something
between two or
more people

snack

a small amount
of food

Read More

Kalman, Bobbie. *When I am Happy.* New York: Crabtree, 2011.

Kawa, Katie. *I Feel Happy.* New York: Gareth Stevens, 2013.

Nelson, Robin. *How Can I Help? A Book about Caring.* Minneapolis: Lerner Publications, 2014.

Index

Photo Credits

The images in this book are used with the permissions of: © L FangXiaNuo/iStock.com, pp. 5, 23 (top left); © Tomwang112/iStock.com, pp. 6–7; © bowdenimages/iStock.com, p. 9; © monkeybusinessimages/iStock.com, pp. 10, 20–21, 23 (bottom left); © Monkey Business Images/Shutterstock.com, pp. 12–13, 23 (top right); © Highwaystarz-Photography/iStock.com, p. 14; © gradyreese/iStock.com, pp. 16–17, 22 (top left); © dolgachov/iStock.com, p. 18; © PeopleImages/iStock.com, p. 22 (top right); © mikkelwilliam/iStock.com, p. 22 (bottom left); © martin-dm/iStock.com, p. 22 (bottom right); © mixetto/iStock.com, p. 23 (bottom right).

Front Cover: © Denis Kuvaev/Shutterstock.com.